GO FACTS ENVIRONMENTAL ISSUES
Water

A & C BLACK • LONDON

Water

contents

WITHDRAWN

First published in Australia by Blake Education Pty Ltd.

This edition published in the United Kingdom in 2007 by
A & C Black Publishers Ltd, 38 Soho Square, London, W1D 3HB.
www.acblack.com

Hardback edition
ISBN 978-0-7136-7963-2

Paperback edition
ISBN 978-0-7136-7971-7

A CIP record for this book is available from the British Library.

Publisher: Katy Pike
Editor: Mark Stafford
Design and layout by The Modern Art Production Group

Image credits: p7 illustration—Toby Quarmby; p20 (b), p21 (all)—Paul McEvoy;
p27 (t)—NASA; p28 (t), p29 (all), rear cover (t)—courtesy World Vision Australia.

Printed in China by WKT Company Ltd.

This book is produced using paper that is made from wood grown in managed sustainable
forests. It is natural, renewable and recyclable. The logging and manufacturing processes
conform to the environmental regulations of the country of origin.

The Rarest Kind of Water

About three-quarters of our planet is covered by water, but almost all of it is salt water. Fresh water doesn't contain salt and only makes up about three per cent of the water on Earth.

Essential fresh water

Fresh water is essential for life. People and animals drink fresh water, and plants need it to grow. We use fresh water for our homes, industry and agriculture.

Most of the world's fresh water is frozen in **glaciers**, **icesheets** and **icecaps**. Glaciers are slow-moving bodies of ice made by the build-up of snow. Icecaps are masses of ice that cover areas of land, and icesheets are very large icecaps. There are massive icesheets in Antarctica and Greenland.

On the surface, under the ground

The rest of the world's fresh water is in lakes and rivers (surface water) and under the ground (**ground water**). Most of the water we use is surface water. Ground water is the result of rain seeping into the ground, and is the source of wells and springs.

Water on the move

The amount of water on our planet never changes, although it continually changes form through the **water cycle**.

However, fresh water can become polluted and unusable by humans. Due to the limited amount of this **resource**, we need to conserve water and stop it from being polluted.

Ground water includes water flowing between rocks and soil, moisture in the soil, frozen soil (permafrost) and underground rivers.

The Water Cycle

The movement of water between the land, the oceans and the atmosphere is called the water cycle.

Three forms

Water can exist in three different forms – solid, liquid or gas. The heat of the sun changes liquid water from oceans, rivers, lakes or melting icecaps into invisible water vapour, which is a gas. This process is called **evaporation**. Water also evaporates from the soil and from the leaves of plants, which is called **transpiration**.

Water up and down

Water vapour rises into the atmosphere. As the vapour rises, it gets colder and changes back into very small water droplets. This change is called **condensation**. The water can freeze into solid ice or snow.

These droplets of water or ice form clouds. When the droplets grow too big and heavy to stay in the air, they fall back to Earth as rain, hail, mist or snow. This is called **precipitation**.

Going underground

Infiltration happens when water soaks into the soil. (Water that doesn't soak into the soil and flows across the ground is called **run-off**.) Some of the water will be soaked up by roots to help plants grow. The rest moves slowly between the soil and rocks as ground water. Ground water eventually flows to the surface again or into the ocean. It is often brought to the surface by man-made wells.

GO FACT!

DID YOU KNOW?

Raindrops are not tear-shaped. Scientists using high-speed cameras have discovered that raindrops resemble the shape of a hamburger bun!

Less precipitation for inland areas
Evaporation from soil and vegetation
Precipitation
Storage in ice and snow
Movement of moist air
Surface run-off
Infiltration
Condensation
Evaporation from lakes and rivers
Storage in lakes
Evaporation from oceans
Storage in oceans
Ground water flow

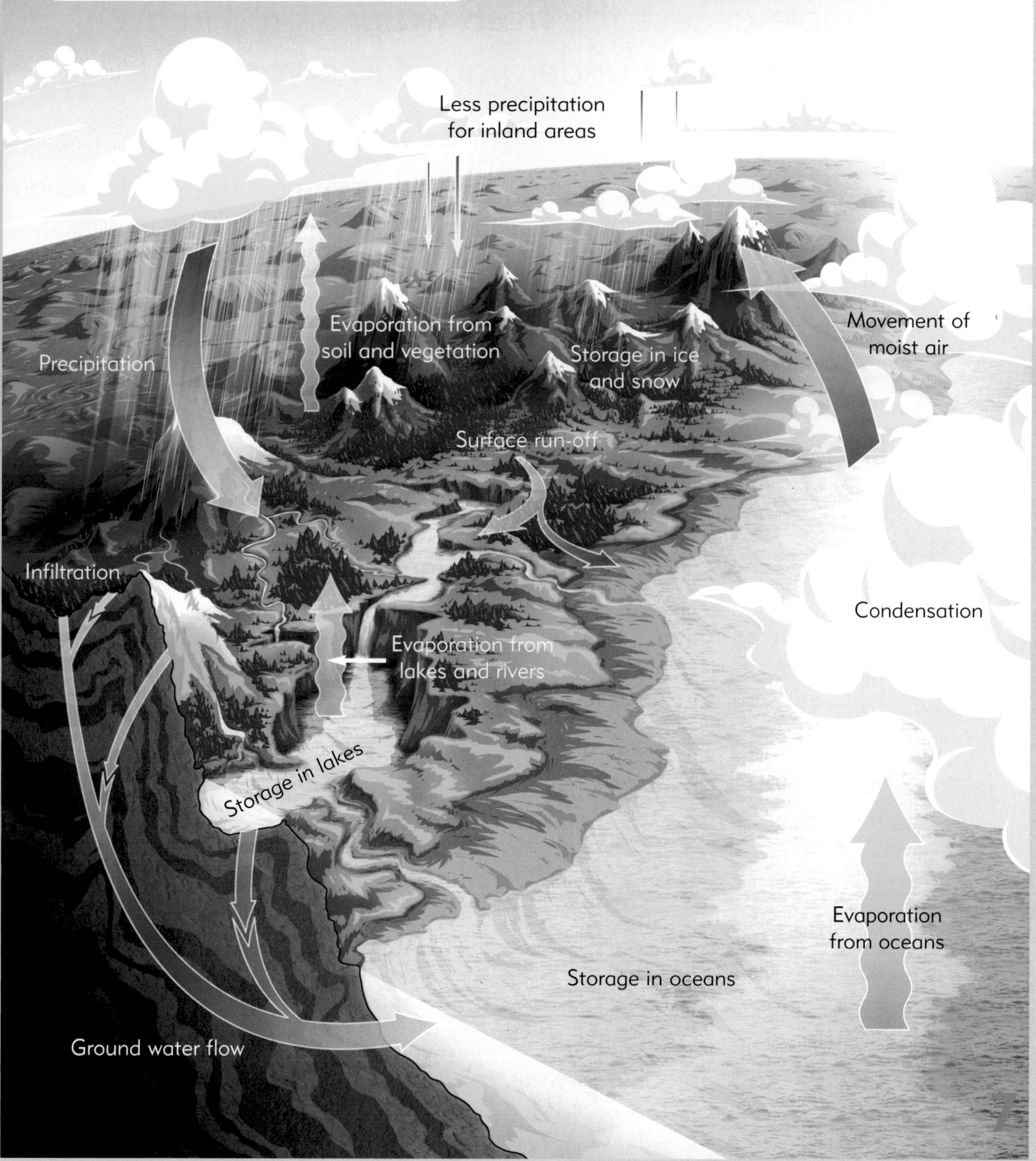

Finding Fresh Water

People access the fresh water stored in rivers, lakes, ice and underground in a variety of ways.

Stored water

Most of the water we use comes from rivers, lakes or reservoirs.

A river starts from melting ice, rainfall or from a lake, and grows as streams in its **catchment area** join it.

Lakes can occur naturally or they can be built. Artificial lakes are known as **reservoirs**. A barrier called a dam is built across a river so water will collect on one side and form a lake. Water is then pumped from the lake through pipes to cities and towns. Sometimes farmers pump water directly from rivers to use on their crops.

Digging for water

An important source of fresh water is ground water. The water collects above a layer of rock that is too dense to allow it to flow through. People dig wells to bring this water to the surface again. Around the world, ground water is the most accessible source of fresh water – about 1.5 billion people use it for their drinking water.

Most of the frozen fresh water is located at the North and South Poles, but this is a long way from where most people live. However, some glaciers partly melt in summer, and the water forms rivers. Many people in China, India, Ecuador, Peru and Bolivia get their fresh water this way.

Icebergs are frozen fresh water floating in saltwater oceans.

Water frozen in glaciers, icecaps and icesheets makes up 70 per cent of the fresh water on Earth.

GO FACT!

DID YOU KNOW?

There are seven rivers in Asia that are fed by glaciers in the Himalayas. These rivers supply water to hundreds of millions of people.

Water and Industry

Water is used for different purposes in many industries. After it has been used, industries must be careful how they dispose of water, so that the environment is not damaged.

Vital for industries

Most water supplied to industries comes from the same sources as household water. Some industries use water for cooling and cleaning, others use water as an ingredient in making food. Water is also used to generate electricity, to mix chemicals and to wash away waste materials.

Factories need fresh water because salt water can damage machinery. The mining, steel, paper and chemical industries use a lot of water.

Dealing with waste water

Industries must follow strict regulations about the safe disposal of waste water. Modern factories have machinery that uses less water and causes less pollution. In some factories, **recycled** water is piped back to the factory after it has been cleaned. Some factories have their own water recycling facilities. This keeps chemicals and industrial waste out of the freshwater supply and out of ground water.

Water is an important part of the process of producing electricity at a nuclear power plant.

Some industries, such as the chemical industry, use and pollute large amounts of water.

GO FACT!

DID YOU KNOW?

Water can generate **hydro-electric** power. Water is released from reservoirs onto **turbines**, which spin to generate electricity. The water is then directed to another reservoir and can be reused. Unlike burning coal to generate electricity, hydro-electric power doesn't produce greenhouse gases.

Water and Agriculture

About 70 per cent of the fresh water we use is for **irrigating** food crops and pasture.

Sprinklers, furrows and drips

There are different ways of irrigating land, some of which use less water than others. The type of irrigation chosen depends on cost, availability of equipment, the type of soil and the crop being grown.

Furrow irrigation allows water to run down pre-dug channels. Sprinkler systems spray water onto a crop. Sprinklers wet the whole plant, not just the roots. This can cause diseases on leaves of the crop.

In very hot climates, or when there is a shortage of water, drip irrigation is used. Water pipes with very small openings are laid along the ground near the plants. Water drips slowly out of the openings to water the roots. Although this is an effective way to use less water, it can only be used in small areas and for certain crops.

Flooding the soil

Some crops, such as rice, grow best when flooded. The soil is prepared for planting, then water is allowed to flood onto it. The rice seedlings are planted and left to mature. The water is then drained from the field and the rice dries before it is harvested.

A pivot sprinkler irrigates large circular fields.

Furrow irrigation is often used for crops planted in rows.

GO FACT!

DID YOU KNOW?

Producing:	Uses this many litres of fresh water:
one sheet of A4 paper	10
one slice of bread	40
one glass of beer	75
one cup of coffee	140
one kilogram of rice	3419
one cotton T-shirt	4100
one pair of leather shoes	8000
one kilogram of beef	15 497
one tonne of aluminium	1 340 000

Water Pollution

Water is polluted by industry, agriculture and communities, making it unfit to drink.

Sources of pollution

The major causes of water pollution are chemicals, **pesticides**, fertilisers, untreated **sewage**, factory waste water and litter in stormwater drains.

When industries return water to the water supply, it can contain chemicals, oils and other **pollutants**.

Too much algae

Farmers use chemical fertilisers and pesticides on their crops. When it rains, some of these chemicals wash into rivers. This can cause algal bloom in lakes and rivers. Algal bloom is the rapid growth of **algae** on the water's surface. It blocks out sunlight and uses up oxygen in the water. Fish and plants need oxygen to live, so algal bloom can kill them. Some algae are poisonous and make the water undrinkable.

Bad rain

When heavily polluted air mixes with the water in clouds, the water falls back to earth as acid rain. Acid rain can make the soil so **acidic** that trees can't grow. Too much acid in lakes and rivers kills fish and frogs. This then affects the waterbird population. Stormwater drains carry rainwater away from cities and towns to reservoirs, rivers and oceans. However, this run-off includes litter from the streets, such as cigarette ends and plastic bags.

Pesticides sprayed from a plane can easily drift into lakes and rivers.

Polluted water greatly increases the risk of diseases such as hepatitis, cholera, dysentery and typhoid.

Each year, plastic waste in water and coastal areas kills up to one million seabirds.

Cigarette ends leach chemicals such as cadmium, lead and arsenic within an hour of contact with water. More than four trillion cigarette ends are dropped as litter every year.

Water and Your Home

Many people in the world enjoy access to lots of clean, fresh water. How does it get to their homes?

Fresh water is pumped from a lake or reservoir to a water filtration plant, where it is filtered to remove weeds, fish and minerals. It is then pumped into storage tanks.

From the storage tanks it moves into underground water **mains**, which carry water to taps in our houses. When we open the tap, the pressure in the pipes pushes the water out. Water pipes can also be connected directly to wells or **boreholes** to provide water to houses that are not connected to the water mains.

Using less

In developed countries, each person uses up to 1000 litres of water every day to drink, cook, wash, flush toilets and water gardens. However, in countries where water is not piped into houses, people use as little as five litres per day.

We cannot drink less water, but we can find ways to use less of it for other things. Some ideas are:

- Repair dripping taps.
- Take a quick shower instead of a bath.
- Wash dishes in a sink, not under a running tap.
- Wash the car with a bucket of water instead of a hose.
- Water the garden at cool times of the day.

Can you think of other ways to conserve water?

Water travels long distances to get to your home.

GO FACT!

DID YOU

Waste water from washing machines, dishwashers, kitchen sinks, baths and showers is called grey water. It can be used instead of fresh water to water the garden.

17

Cleaning Our Drinking Water

Drinking water is water that is safe for people to drink and to use for cooking, washing and bathing. Water needs to be cleaned and purified before it is ready to drink.

Sinking sediment

Water is pumped from a river, lake or reservoir into a tank. A chemical called alum is added to the water so that impurities coagulate, or thicken, into small particles called flocs.

The water is then transferred into a sedimentation tank. The flocs attract dirt and sink to the bottom as sediment. The clear water above the sediment is pumped to the next stage, filtration.

Removing particles

The water is filtered through membranes or layers of sand, gravel or charcoal to remove the tiny particles that have not become sediment. This works in the same way that rocks and soil filter ground water.

The filtered water is then disinfected, often with chlorine, to kill bacteria and any harmful microscopic organisms. In some countries, fluoride is added to the water to help prevent tooth decay.

Fresh water from the sea

Salt water can be turned into drinking water by **desalination**. This process removes salt and other impurities from sea water. It is used in parts of the world where fresh water is scarce, such as Israel.

One way to desalinate sea water is reverse osmosis. This method forces sea water through a membrane under high pressure. The membrane acts like a strainer. It stops salt from passing through, but allows fresh water to go to the other side.

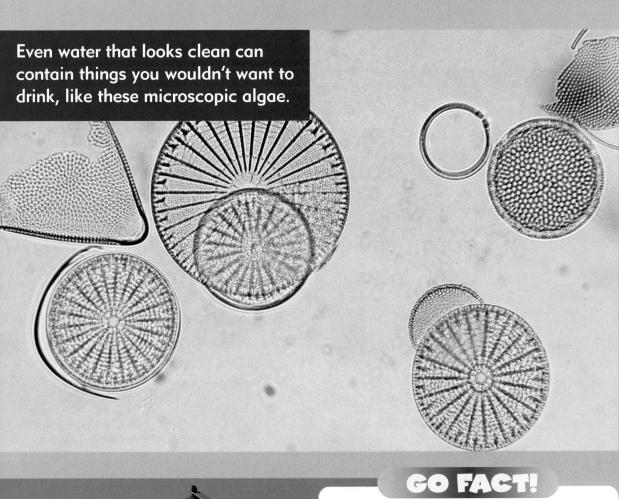

Even water that looks clean can contain things you wouldn't want to drink, like these microscopic algae.

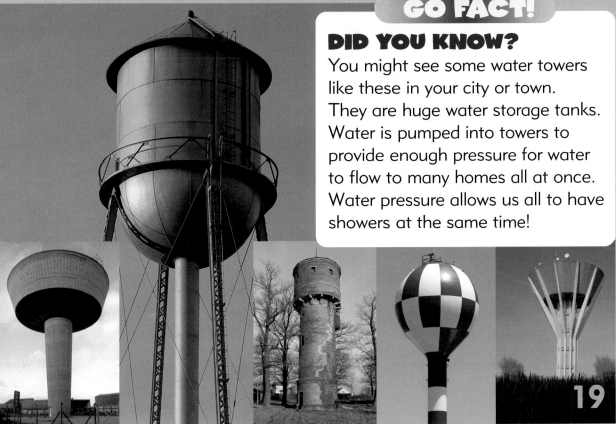

GO FACT!

DID YOU KNOW?

You might see some water towers like these in your city or town. They are huge water storage tanks. Water is pumped into towers to provide enough pressure for water to flow to many homes all at once. Water pressure allows us all to have showers at the same time!

Filter Your Own Water

You can make your own filter to clean water. Remember, filtered water is not safe to drink until it has been purified of germs or bacteria.

You will need:

- two clear containers, such as soft drink bottles
- a funnel (see instructions to make one)
- coffee filter paper or paper towel or a piece of cloth
- gravel, dried beans or crushed eggshells
- sand or uncooked rice
- dirty water (see recipe)

To make a funnel: Curl a piece of paper into a cone shape and tape it together. Make a tiny opening at the bottom for water to drip through.

To make dirty water: Fill one of your containers about halfway with water, and add a spoonful of sand, dust, bits of leaves or grass Shake it up.

You should see cleaner, clearer water after this procedure. Repeat the process with the filtered water to see if it gets clearer. **Do not drink this water!** It may look clean, but it may still contain harmful germs and bacteria.

1 Line the funnel with the coffee filter paper, paper towel or cloth.

2 In the funnel, make a layer of sand or uncooked rice. (You only need one of these.)

3 Make another layer on top of this with the gravel, dried beans or crushed eggshells.

4 Hold the funnel over the empty container. Slowly pour the dirty water into the funnel and watch as it drips through.

Wetlands

A wetland is exactly what the name suggests – wet land. Wetlands help keep the fresh water supply clean and protect the land from floods.

Types of wetland

Wetlands may not be wet all year round, but are wet for long periods. They typically contain shallow water – fresh water, salt water or a mix (called **brackish** water). Examples of wetlands are marshes, mangroves, swamps, bogs and fens.

Wetlands act as natural water filters. They are like sponges, with the soil holding large amounts of water. When there is heavy rain, wetlands absorb the water and then release it slowly later. This helps prevent flooding of the surrounding land.

Dangerous wetlands?

Wetlands were once seen as damp, dangerous places that caused diseases. They were used as dumping grounds for rubbish and sewage, and many wetlands were destroyed to create more land for agriculture and building.

Heavy rain then went straight into rivers, rather than wetlands, and contributed to flooding. Because wetlands are breeding grounds for fish and other aquatic life, the loss of wetlands damaged the fishing industry.

In the UK, it is estimated that only 2.5 per cent of the original wetlands remain, after centuries of intensive farming and building.

Restoration

People have now realised the importance of wetlands and many projects are underway to restore them. This involves clearing weeds and encouraging the growth of native plant species.

Wetlands, like these Kakadu National Park wetlands in northern Australia, occur in every country. Wetlands cover roughly six per cent of the Earth's land surface.

Mangrove wetlands are important breeding grounds for fish and birds.

Many areas in the UK have started campaigns to clean up their local wetlands.

23

The Everglades

The Everglades is a large wetland in southern Florida, USA. It was once a clean wetlands system, but people damaged the natural habitat by changing the flow of water.

Wet summer, dry winter

Water in the Everglades flowed and dried up in a natural cycle. After summer rains, the Everglades flowed steadily to the ocean as a body of water about 200 kilometres long and 80 kilometres wide, but less than 30 centimetres deep. The area was known as the *River of Grass*.

In the past, after the rains there were six months of dry weather. Alligators built their nests above the water level. Migrating waterbirds ate the plants that had been underwater in summer and the fish that had moved into shallow pools.

Shrinking wetland

As people needed more land, canals were built to control floods and drain the Everglades for agriculture and drinking water. The Everglades shrank to half its original size and the regular flow of water stopped. The water became polluted by fertilisers and pesticides. Sometimes, water was released into the Everglades in winter. This flooded the dry areas in the wrong season, destroying alligator nests and scattering the food of migrating birds.

Redirecting the water

The people of Florida realised that they needed a healthy Everglades for a healthy environment. Since 1993, water flow has been increased and marsh filtering systems have been built to clean the water. In the future more fresh water will be captured and redirected to the parts of the Everglades that need it most.

GO FACT!

DID YOU KNOW?

The Everglades National Park is the only place in the world where alligators and crocodiles exist side by side.

The Everglades is home to the Great Blue Heron and Florida Panther.

The *River of Grass* still supplies water to major cities such as Miami.

Dams

A dam is a barrier built to stop the flow of water. Dams have been built since ancient times to store water and to prevent rivers from flooding. However, building dams also disrupts **ecosystems** and the lives of people.

Benefits

Early, simple dams worked by blocking water flow in a stream with soil and branches. Reservoirs were dug alongside the stream or river, and channels built to direct the water into the reservoir. Water was pumped or carried to homes and farmland.

Modern dams are enormous. They not only control flooding and provide a reliable supply of drinking water, but the water can also be used to irrigate crops and generate hydro-electricity. People also use them for recreation, such as boating and waterskiing.

Damage

A large dam is expensive and takes many years to build. Dams flood a lot of land that could be used for housing or agriculture. Some people have to move because their land will become flooded. This affects their homes and farms, their jobs and food.

Dams also have negative effects on the environment. They can disrupt ecosystems in and around rivers and stop the natural flow of water into wetlands.

waterskis

The Aswan High Dam in Egypt was built to prevent the Nile River flooding, generate electricity and provide water for agriculture. It has created a huge reservoir behind the dam wall.

Reservoir

Dam

Nile River

Fort Peck Dam in Montana, USA, can hold approximately 23 billion litres of water!

GO FACT!

DID YOU KNOW?

The Three Gorges Dam in China will flood the homes of more than one million people – but will also control floods further down the Yangtze River.

27

Water for Everyone?

All humans need water to survive. In modern, developed countries, clean water is easy to find – we simply turn on a tap. In some countries, water is a luxury. More than one billion people in the world do not have access to clean, safe water.

Not enough water

In the **developing world**, many people cannot get enough water for drinking and cooking. If they can find water, they may have to carry it long distances from rivers and wells. Women and children spend a large part of every day fetching water. This prevents them from doing important work and going to school.

If there is a drought, there is no water to collect.

Dirty water kills

Where there is no running water, people don't have flushing toilets and sewerage systems. Human and animal waste ends up in rivers and can cause diseases. Every day about 6 000 people in the developing world, mostly children under the age of five, get sick and die from drinking polluted water.

The United Nation's Millennium Development Goals call for the number of people who don't have sustainable access to safe drinking water and basic **sanitation** to be halved by the year 2015. This big goal can be achieved if governments make water and sanitation a funding priority for the world's poorest people.

Drinking dirty water from a polluted spring can cause diseases like cholera, diarrhoea and dysentery.

A capped spring provides constant fresh water.

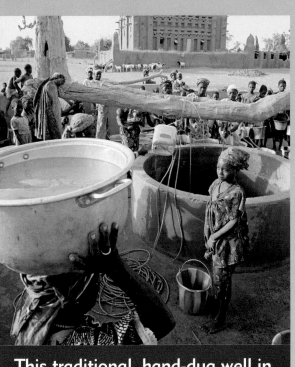

This traditional, hand-dug well in Mali isn't deep enough to reach a steady supply of water.

A protected well and pump supplies clean water to students of Shambarai Primary School in Tanzania.

29

Top 10 Water Facts

Most rainy days	Up to 350 rainy days per year at Mount Waialeale, Hawaii, USA.	
Fewest rainy days	1 day every 6 years in Arica, Chile.	
Most rain in one day	1.87 metres at Chilaos, La Réunion.	
Tallest dam	The Rogun Dam in Tajikistan is 335 metres high.	
Biggest iceberg	Before the Antarctic B15 iceberg broke into pieces, it was 295 kilometres long and 37 kilometres wide – about the same size as Jamaica.	
Longest river	The Nile is 6670 kilometres long, running through Tanzania, Uganda, Sudan and Egypt.	
Highest waterfall	Angel Falls in Venezuela is 979 metres high.	
Deepest ocean	The Mariana Trench in the Pacific Ocean is almost 11 kilometres deep.	
Worst flood	The Huang He River flooded in China in 1931, killing 3 700 000 people.	
Fastest person on water	Donald Campbell reached 444.71 km/h on Lake Dumbleyung, Australia, in 1964.	

Glossary

algae very simple plants that grow in or near water

acidic containing an acid. An acid has a sour taste, and reacts with a base to form a salt.

borehole a hole drilled deep into the earth to release water or oil

brackish slightly salty

catchment area land that catches rainwater which then drains into a river or dam

condensation the process of changing from a gas to a liquid

desalination the process of removing the salt from saltwater leaving drinkable, fresh water

developing world the nations of the world which are less economically and technologically advanced

ecosystem a community of species interacting with each other and the environment

evaporation the process of liquid becoming a vapour

glacier slow-moving body of ice made by the build-up of snow

ground water water beneath the Earth's surface

hydro-electric relating to the generation of electricity from falling water

icecap a mass of ice that permanently covers a large area of land

icesheet a very large icecap. The only icesheets currently are in Greenland and Antarctica.

infiltration the slow seepage of water from the Earth's surface down through open spaces and pores in the ground

irrigate to water land to grow crops

mains the network of pipes that move water from a local station to individual homes

pesticide a chemical used to kill pests, such as insects and rodents

pollutant waste that contaminates water, air or soil

precipitation any form of water that falls from clouds: rain, snow, hail, sleet or mist

recycled having been used before

reservoir a place where water is collected and stored

resource a material that is valuable in its relatively natural form.

run-off water from rain, melted snow or other sources that flows across the ground, rather than soaking into the soil

sanitation the way that water and waste is handled to protect people's health

sewage human waste

transpiration the release of water vapour from the leaves of plants

turbines a motor through which liquid or gas flows in order to produce power

water cycle the movement of water between land, oceans and the atmosphere

Index